Free Verse Editions
Edited by Jon Thompson

A SHORT HISTORY OF ANGER

Joy Manesiotis

Winner of the New Measure Poetry Prize

Parlor Press
Anderson, South Carolina
www.parlorpress.com

Parlor Press LLC, Anderson, South Carolina 29621

Library of Congress Cataloging-in-Publication Data on File

978-1-64317-367-2 (paperback)
978-1-64317-368-9 (pdf)
978-1-64317-369-6 (ePub)

1 2 3 4 5

Cover design by Margaret Buchanan
Cover photograph by Patrik Stollarz
Author photo by William Vasta

Parlor Press LLC is an independent publisher of scholarly and trade titles in print and
multimedia formats. This book is available in paperback and ebook formats from Parlor
Press on the web at https://parlorpress.com or through online and brick-and-mortar
bookstores. For submission information or to find out about Parlor Press publications,
write to Parlor Press, 3015 Brackenberry Drive, Anderson, South Carolina 29621, or
email editor@parlorpress.com.

~For those who perished and those who survived

And in memory,

 ~Brigit Pegeen Kelly, whose hand is everywhere here

 ~Catherine Caloyer Mason, whose family would speak

Ζωή σε εμάς

Contents

A Short History of Anger

Now it is common to speak about the catastrophe of war. However, something that weighs heavier in your guts is the sudden extermination of a fully alive world, with its lights, with its shadows, with its rituals of joy and sorrow, with the tightly woven net of its life.

—George Sepheris
A Poet's Journal: Days of 1945-1951

And will there be enough birds to send messages to all the dead?

And who will write the messages with their tears?

And who will sing the laments? And wash the bones in wine?

———————————————

Some say clockwise, some say tipped away from the handle

but *quick flick of wrist*, she flipped the cup upside down on the saucer, laughing,
circled the cup in the air three times

                    —first, brew the coffee thick and dark and sweet:

and sit together, the women,

                —first: warm the water in the briki, spoon coffee and sugar

                    first: allow the coffee to sink, then stir

and heat until the coffee foams up

                    —and lift from the stove,

and it foams again

                    —and lift again—

until it is steaming in each cup, and you

                    —sit together

and finally, the cup lifted away, the grounds painted down the sides:

Ah, she would say, *you have bad luck in your future. Ah*, she would say, *you must go
home.*

Ah, she would say, *there is happiness flying toward you. There is a bird.
The grave must be cleaned. A marriage ring. There is money.*

•

Suite One

Smyrna: a city of all those lights. *Catastrophe*

How to convey the Greek sense
of the word (of any word):
Catastrophe,

the moment in history—*history*—

to we who have no history, no
sense of history,

how it gets planted
in the blood, and then passed on,

who have no sense of blood

how the *Catastrophe* set up shop
in the psyche of the Greek people,

opened its awnings, set out its tables and chairs
in the late afternoon light, everyone
just waking from the midday rest—

•

They had been driven into the sea, Smyrna burning,
driven—hardly prepared:

•

—is it possible to be prepared to be massacred?—

—like cattle, dogs (can you hear that inflection?)

into the harbor water
after days of waiting at the edge, their homes torched—horses, sabers, fire—no food,
no money—

that cousin dismembered, this sister beheaded—
their bodies still lying where they fell

*—(easy to feel immured, to think nothing of this, those of you
who have been able to bury your dead)*

—a history of panic, blood—

waiting for the British ships at anchor

*—to offer harbor
as in* katafighios: *shelter*

as in thousands of Greek people—Ottoman subjects, Orthodox, Christian—
dying in the water around them, while the naval officers looked on, and

did nothing, nothing,

*—típota,
the word means nothing, less than nothing*

•

The crows know. The crow is talking.

(Many of them were actually in the underworld.)

        —What happens when a member of your family, an ancestor, was dismembered?

On the beach, a crow eating the dead body of a murrelet;
bird eating a bird. Same
stony eyes in the crow.

What gets passed along the nerve pathways,

Between sips at the murrelet's body.

and how does it travel, generation to generation,
and how does it mutate?

More than small stories of childhood
planted in memory: transgressions, traumas:
a set of histories,

                            —History with a big H,
                                 ash in the mouth,

a more petty form of protection.

                        •

—imprinted in the blood, spooled around the genes, travelling along nerve pathways,
out and out,
ash in the mouth, heat waves

•

—a history of invasion, inversions, what can happen now?

•

11

The Chorus Considers the City Before the Destruction

—*Smyrna: major port town of Anatolia. A city of X Turks, X Greeks, X Armenians, X Jews:*
Or no, X Muslims, X Orthodox Christians, all Ottoman subjects.

—*A city that held its long history: Greek, Roman, Ottoman: a city that held all their cultures:*
European, cultured, prosperous:

—*waterfront lined with shady café gardens, tavernas, brasseries:*

—*Turkish cafés, Armenian patisserie: roasted cinnamon, apple smoke*

—*Greeks who spoke Turkish, Turks who spoke Greek, all who spoke French:*

—*music: rembetika, Smyrna style, whole families in the cafes at night*

•

(how much shock can be tolerated, and how much will you
not register it?

is it proportional? those of us who
have never experienced such a thing: is it imaginable, really,

when you—I—can walk away, forget about it
while at dinner with friends, pasta steaming on the table? if you don't

have to live it—or live with it—how far
can imagination go? when do you

                                        •

—*rein it in, no, don't look, just before allowing the image to rise up fully and take shape?*)

                                        •

allegiances having switched, *very sorry, we forgot to tell you*

                                        •

                                        —*very sorry, very sorry,*
                        this poem beginning to flounder under the weight of all its history,

                                        but who could hold it up?

—————————

I carried my baby, the town on fire, horse hooves
down the cobblestone street, closer, as if with each sound
the horses grew larger, the soldiers more fierce, the sabers growing
with each strike of hoof, rushing down on us, everything bigger, bigger.

—It is impossible to speak of such things.

I will say I held the baby's face
against my chest, afraid he would cry, afraid I would smother him:
what fear was born into his body that day? What
anger pressed into his small form? How would he live his life through it,
if he had a life? What happens when a cry is smothered in that way?

Never did I think they would set the fire upon us.

And on my husband's back, his mother, frozen in stroke.

In this way, we tried to make our way down the street.

———————————

Oranía?

Ζωή σε εμάς   May her memory be eternal.   *—She died as a baby.*

Iannis?

Ζωή σε εμάς   May his memory be eternal.   *—He died.*

Stella?

—She died of the typhoid fever.
She was twelve.

Ζωή σε εμάς   May her memory be eternal.

Panayotis?

—The older one got away. The younger?
He died.

Ζωή σε εμάς   May his memory be eternal.

Iakovos?

—He got away.

Nikos?

—They buried him alive.

Ζωή σε εμάς   May his memory be eternal.

Tonis?

—He lived.

Haroula?

Haroula?

Gregory?

—The army.
Then he died.

Ζωή σε εμάς   May his memory be eternal.

Hariklea?

—Για την Αμερική
She left to America.
Before.

The Chorus Considers the Matter of Numbers

—*Smyrna: major port town of Anatolia. A city of X Turks, X Greeks, X Armenians, X Jews.*

—*The ratio of Christian population to Muslim population a matter of dispute,*

—*(Greeks numbered 320,000)*

but the city was a multi-ethnic center—until September 1922.

—*According to X: 1919-1922, the Greeks in Smyrna outnumbered Turks two to one: 150,000, half the population.*

—*According to Y: before World War I, Greeks numbered 130,000 out of a population of 250,000.*

—*According to the Ottoman census of 1905: 100,356 Muslims, 73,636 Orthodox Christians, 11,127 Armenian Christians, and 25,854 others.*

—*According to the U.S. Ambassador to the Ottoman Empire: more than half of Smyrna's population was Greek.*

—*According to the American Consul General in Smyrna: Before the fire: 400,000 people lived in the city: 165,000 Turks, 150,000 Greeks, 25,000 Jews, 25,000 Armenians, and 20,000 foreigners— 10,000 Italians, 3,000 French, 2,000 British, and 300 Americans.*

—According to the scholars: prior to the Destruction, Smyrna had more Greeks than Athens, the capital of Greece.

—According to the Ottomans: it was Infidel Smyrna.

—Why?
All the Greeks.

Suite Two

—Wait: we have to:

•

A mother, whose mother came from Smyrna
and left the year before the Destruction

whose brothers, in turn, were dismembered, buried alive,
who went back to get one out of prison, but he was underground by then,

—literally,

whose own mother had come to visit and stayed the rest of her life—
Hariklea, for whom you were named—

no home to return to, burned behind her, no
money, no photos, no children, sisters, parents to return to

the Destruction, a *catastrophe*,
that set up shop in her blood, brought out its tables and chairs,

and she sat, drinking her Greek coffee, reading the grounds,
cup turned over, Smyrna burning and burning

•

—And what has it cost you—a burden in the blood—

or what do you carry now: but perhaps that question is off key
the real questions being unformed, unuttered, unable to be uttered

•

21

The Chorus Considers the City Before the Destruction, Again

—Newspapers: 11 Greek; 7 Turkish; 5 Armenian; 4 French; 5 Hebrew

"In the evenings, maids would sweep the dust from the street, place armchairs outside the houses. Everyone came out after supper and offered cakes and sweets to their neighbors and friends."

In the harbor, thirty-three steamboat companies, passenger ships each day: London, Marseilles, Genoa, Constantinople

—Turkish cafés, Armenian patisserie, Greek tavernas: Greek game pies, Yorkshire pudding, boeuf á la mode, baklava and kataifi

Armenian agents, German traders, English mill owners

—Less "Turk" and "Greek" than Muslim, Orthodox Christian, all Ottoman subjects: neighbors, friends, schoolmates

Swiss hoteliers, Dutch fig merchants, Austrian tailors, Greek bankers

"At Christmas, we'd sing carols in French, Greek, English, and Italian."

•

You recognize that shape. It stands in the air,
only slightly darker, no outline. It wants

to talk to you, but you turn away. You can't listen
to its lament. The weight it carries is heavy, but you cannot

help lift it.

•

—But you must.

•

The holy water would not tip from the bottle
even though she poured it and poured it,
the clear liquid rocked and shivered in you, as blue as the bottle
as she rocked and remembered, and told the story, in hushed voice
in the blue of dusk: her whisper hissing across the air,
the curse, the evil eye, searching to find you:

the holy water would not bless the house, and so the house must be left
the house would not be blessed and so must be left
the water would not pour from the narrow blue neck
it rocked backward inside the bottle
the bottle blue, her rocking backward as she told the story
drawing back as if struck

—The story its own protection, the telling a net to hold you,
woven to protect you

•

—We don't talk family business outside the family.

•

Her face outlined in the blue of dusk, in profile, a cameo cut into the falling light.

•

The knife? It was from Constantinople.

———————————————

—Never did you think they would set fire upon you. Smoke at the edge of town,
the uncle saying rest now, there is time.

Quiet in the street. Smoke at the edge of the town, outside the town, in the hills. Never
did you believe they would set the fire upon you.

My mother had a stroke. That moment, as the Turks flooded the streets, horses clattering, torches in hand. That moment, she froze, slumped, her limbs locked up. And the baby, crying—trying to shush him. We were to make our way to the house of our Russian friends, brave enough to shelter us. We—reviled, for what? Because we were Greek, Christian, no other.

·

*—Yes, you think "clattering" too common, not original enough,
but what is language to this experience? Does it matter
which words fail, exactly? Will a more arresting word rescue these people, save them
from Smyrna burning inside them?*

The Chorus Considers the Politicians

*—All military operations, international decisions, trades
made by the British, French, the Allies in World War I:*

*help us now
and we will give you this land—
the Ottomans will fall, with your help—*

*(and the Italians have left the table...)
(it is a big idea...)*

•

*—In the harbor, twenty battleships: British, French, American:
Broadcasting music to mask the sound of screaming: people on the quay, in the water*

•

*—H Megali Ithea—The Big Idea—
Greece could recover its land from the Assyrians,
a land for all Greeks, Strabo, the ancient geographer, wrote:*

*from Sicily to Asia Minor to the Black Sea, Macedonia,
Crete and Cyprus,*

•

a restoration,

but what failure of imagination was it, exactly?—

———————————

I am afraid of the dirt coming down on my face, of my fingernails continuing to grow, of the air slowly filtering away: a stream, then a wisp, then an occasional slight stirring. But I can slip away, I can sink down into the letting go, and here, I am traveling: across great expanse, the open prospect, even though storm clouds sit at the horizon and stream toward me, across a landscape I do not know—barren, but unlike the rock outcroppings, the dusty plains of Smyrna—the sky a burnished pewter. Yet I ride toward it. And the wideness pours around me, I move through it as a fish moves through water, and I am free. I do not care that they have buried me while I still breathe—what was left of that life? Why am I afraid? I am less so here, as the breath winnows away, as the dirt fills my nostrils, I will not scrabble for this life. I am done. I am traveling.

And who will wash the graves each day?

And who will make the grave?

And who will sing the *moiroloía* to help the souls cross over?

———————————————

The Chorus Considers the Torching of Smyrna

—Fire that swept up the streets of the Greek quarter, climbing the spars of the houses,
running along the porches, across roof lines, the barge rafters, tracing the outlines of the houses,
drawing the skeleton in flames.

—And the ash, the soot, rising in flags above the rooflines, the books, rugs, couches
sending ash and particles and wisps of horsehair, paper, wood turned to ash, smoke
filled with ash that settled back down as the flames subsided to embers,
crackling ash that drifted/sailed/glided/coasted
back to settle on the spars, the scaffolding, the few upright spears, the skeleton.

The person who does the murder seems large.
As if large. Much faster. Able to swoop down.
As if larger. Larger than all of us. Larger than a family, a community.
Just one of them.

But really, they were small. Small people. Very short.

It is not that the streets were filled with the sound of the women wailing, after all the dead, after all the fire, smoke rising in mute flags above the rubble. You might think the air was full of keening. But it was not. It was the absence of the keen, the air still, no disturbance, the utter silence of it.

Smoke? It makes no sound.

Suite Three

Some say clockwise, some say tipped away from the handle

but *quick flick of wrist*, she flipped the cup upside down on the saucer, laughing,
circled the cup in the air three times

> *—first, brew the coffee thick and dark and sweet:*

and sit together, the women,

> *—first: warm the water in the briki, spoon coffee and sugar*
>
> *first: allow the coffee to sink, then stir*

and heat until the coffee foams up

> *—and lift from the stove,*

and it foams again

> *—and lift again—*

until it is steaming in each cup, and you

> *—sit together*

and finally, the cup lifted away, the grounds painted down the sides:

Ah, she would say, *you have bad luck in your future. Ah*, she would say, *you must
go home.*

Ah, she would say, *there is happiness flying toward you. There is a bird.*
The grave must be cleaned. A marriage ring. There is money.

•   •   •

You are so much larger than we are now,
who are wedded to our small pities

but you are expansive,

                                        —*beyond longing,*

over us

                                        —*cloud cover, stardust,*

absorbing all our yearning:

                                        —*blanket of fog, rain, wide sky*

•

At Easter, a bath of red dye and vinegar on the stove, we dye the eggs, dozens—

and make the *tsoureki*: cinnamon, *mastiha*, orange zest: knead and rise,

                                        —*and rise again,*

                        —*enacting resurrection, rising up and rising up,*

and we braid the bread, and braid in red eggs,

37

After we have oiled the eggs, after the bread is taken from the oven,
and the lamb from the spit, feta and olives on the table

we each hold an egg and crack it against another's egg:

—they crack open the tomb

we ask for luck. We ask for blessing.

•

You (I) recognize that shape. It stands in the air,
only slightly darker, no outline. It wants

to talk to you (me). I listen
to its lament. The weight it carries is heavy

and you (I) must help lift it.

•

My cousins say they were made to pray in the closet with the icons. Our
grandmother told them the *iconostasia* were crying.

•

All my uncles could dance.

•

Sometimes the beads, *koumboloi*, would click, one at a time, through someone's fingers.

•

They were closed in there with the crying icons, the flat Byzantine faces, outlined in gold leaf. I don't know if they saw any crying. I don't know if they did any crying.

•

Sometimes the *koumboloi* would fly around the hand, and click together all at once, a sense of arrival—as they landed, together,

in the palm: *swish and click, swish and click,*

marking the thinking, giving it shape and weight in the air.

•

It didn't happen to me.

•

The soup will last three days

The walk to the street car will take ten minutes.

There will be a store.

•

In summer, the *koumboloyia* were placed around the table, at each person's place. And a drink: *metaxa*. The cards in the middle.

•

The body is laid out, pristine in the coffin, made up and dressed. The old women are in the corner. The old women:

—*They are missing teeth.*

They rock. And sing. They are dressed in black.

—*So is everyone else.*

The body is laid out for two nights and everyone comes to pay their respects. On the third day, the body will be buried, in time for bodily resurrection. The *moiroloía*, the lament, the old women know it in their bones, they tear their hair, they rock back and forth. They keen.

•

She is so much larger than we are now,
who are wedded to our small pities

but she is expansive,

—*beyond longing,*

over us

—*cloud cover, stardust,*

absorbing all our yearning:

—*blanket of fog, rain, wide sky*

•

—*May her memory be eternal*

My uncle left the basement of the Russians' house each day, as if
he filtered through the wall, materialized on the street. One Turkish man

opened his store, sold bread, supplies, to the ghosts
who slipped in, counting out their few coins.

—He made money on the displaced.

We waited through the still air of afternoon, its boredom,
for my uncle's step on the threshold, the small bit of food. I never asked

if he walked as if he were not hunted. The day his form did not fill the room,
and the light on the house across the lane sharpened through the afternoon

and then, slowly went out, I imagined him walking eternally

—may his memory—

in the streets of Smyrna,

—shadows falling across his shoulders.

—What left behind?
ash in the mouth

And the silence that settled in their bones, they carried it there,
the deep hollow, the marrow. It stopped them from speaking,

the silence kept them. They held the *moiroloía* in their bones
with the silence, a muteness, the uncoupling from their lives.

And the birds? Their shadows swept over the right shoulders of those who lived,
startling across their bodies, their line of sight.

●

—Only the carrion birds stayed, the ones
not permitted to cross over.

—As his breath slips away, will a great wind let loose across the rocky plain?

The Chorus Considers Epigenetics

—Let me study your affliction:

—Ash in the mouth: methyl groups attaching, pollen sticky along the double-helix
DNA's strand, tightly wound, or loose, around histone spools:

The wisteria blooms sudden, all swagger, no foliage, the violet disks of petals shattering down
the face of air.   The fire blooms, rains ash.

The scent heavy in the mouth.   ~~Not ash, sweet.   But heavy~~. Bruise.   Ornament.

Methylation:
powder holding fast to scaffolding, molecular scars

The *I-have-nothing-to-draw-on* emptiness, the no place to turn, the *I-will-save-my-own-skin*, half-turn, in the darkened room,

> —*Your chest a small house fear has built, a hut on the ice, small fire, bundled figure*
> *huddled over a line sent down into the frozen lake*

The Chorus Considers Fate

The Chorus wants to talk to you:

Your ancestors are standing in a circle. We have made the circle very wide.

When now, years later, even a small shade of comment takes shape as threat,
when the step from *threat* to *safe* is only a small one, but one you cannot take,

and moonlight casts the sleeping world in silver while you pace the house

—mirrors of unrest, yard sloping away—

> *you recognize that shape. It stands in the air,*
> *only slightly darker, no outline. It wants*
>
> *to talk to you, but you turn away. You cannot listen*
> *to its lament. The weight it carries is heavy, but you cannot*
>
> *(you must) help lift it.*

The knife was from Constantinople. It had been quiet a long time. It had stopped talking. For a long time, it had laid on the sideboard. Silent. For a long time. It was a dagger, a long curved blade. It was from Constantinople.

Around the table glasses of *metaxa*, cigarette smoke, worry beads. On the sideboard, the knife, its hilt of worked stone, ivory, celadon, ruby, its curved blade quiet, not talking, everyone else talking, slapping cards,

and in the room above them, we ran across their ceiling, back and forth, a game my cousins played, like a wave back and forth, the ocean talking outside, the glint on the coil of waves out the window,

we were at the window, looking down across the sand, its dun color stretching out, the night falling on the sand, and back and forth, we ran.

And they played cards, the adults, slapping cards, their laughter waves across our floor. We passed by the knife in the day. It never talked. The blade sheathed in beaten metal, inlaid stones. The knife was from Constantinople.

The *metaxa*. The clicking of worry beads. Their throaty laughter. Their shouts. The slapping of cards.

Then it stopped, everything silent, eerie. We froze, mid-flight across the room. Maybe the knife was talking now. But we couldn't hear it. Each cousin froze, curls stopped in midair, arms rising through air halted in flight.

The knife was in his thigh, she had buried it in his thigh, the worked hilt of beautiful stone against his skin, and blood, there must have been blood, the silence in waves against the walls.

We could hear only the absence of the adults' voices, our grandmother's hand leaving the knife, her friend's blood. A dark humming the air. There must have been blood. Her name, murmured, a small buzzing.

*—May their memories
be eternal.*

The Chorus Considers the Population Exchange

—October, 1922: one month after Smyrna, Eastern Thrace: evacuated.

—The Greek point of view: the only hope of avoiding the collapse of the Greek state and humanitarian disaster was to find a place to settle the incoming refugees as quickly as possible.

—The Turkish point of view: the victorious nationalist Turks had no place for Christian minorities, but they wanted to expel them on terms the rest of the world would accept.

—In Lausanne, all parties tried to absolve themselves of responsibility. Everyone realized the idea of compulsory exchange was shameful. But they all, secretly, desired it.

—50,000 Muslim Turks were exchanged for 1.3 million Christian Greeks:

—You can't live here anymore because you are the wrong religion.

—Let's be clear: This was not repatriation: It was the uprooting of people from their homelands on both sides. Ethnic cleansing done by diplomatic plan.

—Nation-states do not have the right to exchange their citizens. They are not cattle. They are not sheep. They are human beings. It is against the major principles of international law.

—And then a burst of laughter, the adults laughing, a surge lifting you
back to your wave of play.

—You could hear only your grandmother's hand leaving the knife:

dry skin of her fingers brushing cool hemispheres
of garnet, jade, the cut surfaces of rubies, emeralds. The air

rushing past, whispering, as her hand lifted, left the handle
& its beautiful density, its worked surface,

   —years of someone's attention on its beauty, years of someone's hand against the stones,

blade in its sheath, knife snug against his waist. Hooves against cobblestone.
The knife riding against the warmth of his torso, his hip.

It was a wind, that sound, the air moving across her skin, voices
carried across the rocky plain,

                    —murmur and hiss: urgent with request.

                    —Her brother was speaking, dirt filling his mouth.

We could hear only that sound. There must have been others: laughter dying away,
ringing against the walls, bright in overhead light.

                    —Was someone wailing?

We heard only the wind, the voices

                    —Did a keen lift in the air? Quiet and far off, someone wailing?

And if the playhouse door remains open, which animals will venture out?

And if the child's body is found nailed to a door, whose back will carry that weight?

And if the sunlight falls slant across the table, whose name will be spoken out loud?

—May her memory be eternal.

The Chorus Considers the Population Exchange, Again

—We are a wide voice.

—The Chorus wants to talk to you. It wants to tell you the story.

—And then you will rotate under its weight.

—The Chorus wants to talk to you: Your ancestors are standing in a circle.
They have made the circle very wide.

•

"You leave your home, your possessions, your memories, your youth—you leave
your dead there . . . it is not easy."

—There is no Smyrna now.

"When we arrived in Greece, we were hungry and thirsty. Our children were dying
of starvation in our arms. And what did we get by coming here? Nothing, just
trouble . . ."

—And how important is "story" to your understanding? How important is "story"
to this telling?

"My mother's grandmother left 800 poems in Cretan dialect, written with Arabic
letters."

Suite Four

—*When your home changes behind you, a series of doors*
closing, a hallway of doors

When your home closes behind you, blotted out,
and the past becomes

ghost or *ghost town* or *ghosted,*

—*the verb*—

as if erased,
as if smudged: an eraser pulled across paper, pastel chalk rubbed,

—*as in rubbed out,*

but no—drawn with intention:
a softer line, a thinner area of color, the paper bleeding
through, edges blurred, the form indistinct,

—*ghosted*

as if you could see through the town, the house, the friends,
the cobblestone steps, the church:

—*all a thin scrim now, barely there.*

•

Only the ghost of the *psalti* chants,
the call of the *muezzin* an echo of the psalti's wail, the chant

winding through the call to prayer,

—atonal, pentatonic—

rising up the steps of its prayer,

—smoke in the air

frankincense fragrant and blue, smoke in the air

•

Not solid, not a place to return to,

all the snapshots of that life only in memory, not
to be trusted—memory

—unstable, capricious, changeable—

will hold up images that were never there

—chimeras of moments, distorted, changed—

And if you
were to return, or try to return,

—you would be a stranger there now,
what did you think?—

your home inhabited by other people, who speak
another language,

—using your cups, sleeping in your bed.

—If your home is still there, not burned to the ground, smoking.

•

Which would be worse? All burned, destroyed? Or intact, but used
by the *other*, your intimate things handled each day?

—Your favorite coffee cup, your sheets, your chairs.

And each time one of them,

—them

lifts a cup, runs a hand across the red velvet sofa,

a door slams shut

—again and again—

door after door slamming

or locking carefully with a click of the tumbler,

—so quiet, just the chk-chk *of falling into place—*

until there stands a hallway of doors
between you and your home:

—*shut.*

•

The Chorus Considers the Population Exchange, Again

"I am from Smyrna. I will always be from Smyrna."

—If your name is written somewhere, it is possible someone will find it.

"There were 375 Greek houses and 100 Turkish houses, one next to the other. Neighbors, villagers were separated in tears . . . the whole village was in tears when they left."

If your name is written somewhere, it is possible someone will find it.

"We shared our houses with them. We gave a part of our land to them, so they could live."

Because that hand is not yours, or the hand
                              of someone in your family. Because that hand

is perhaps not clean. Because that hand
is not yours or the hand of someone in your family,
                              and looks instead upon your belongings

as plunder, as possessions of the *other*—or perhaps, as salvation—

                                        •

A murder of crows: mobbing in the tree: calling to the dead: calling
over the dead:

                                        •

                                        —and so, might be sullied.

                                        •

or no, calling to eat the dead—or calling to protect
the living

                                        —to celebrate their feast: smart birds,

                                        •

Because the things represent your life,

•

—announcing their find, their victory

•

because that hand did not work for days to acquire those cups, did not

•

A murder of crows, but who are they calling? Mobbing, black mist
in the tree, dust sliding from their slick feathers, a murder

•

work all day, each day, to build this house, but instead walked into it

as a spoil of war, what can it know of
the walls, the tapestries, the rugs?

—Of the hours of laughter and song in this parlor?

Of the grandmother who died in this bed?

Of the rembetika and sweet cakes, the holy water and jewels?

———————————————

The Chorus Considers Fate, Again

—Unturning.

—Atropos.

—It sweeps in like that:
unturning:

or: turning: away or other.

Your ancestors are standing in a circle. They have made the circle very wide.

Is this "enemy?" What is "enemy?"

Doubled: the refugees: doubled,
connected to those whose lives they step into, by what has been torn away.

—It will reach you. Whatever you do will only bring it closer.
And then you will rotate under its weight.

—You push back against it.

Palms upturned, shoulders lifted for a moment:
each moment weighed: Snip, snip.

Because the light was actually moonlight, slanting in rectangles
across the wall of the house, the shapes of plants in the yard.
Because time stretches outward with no limit.
Because the humming in the air has only surfeit and no cease.
Because fatigue pushes down on my eyelids. Because my voice is faint.
Because all is stillness outside.
Because my dreams are invaded by an other's dreams.
Because a life can be ended so suddenly.
Because my fears are often pedestrian.

Each day, the streetcar, the butcher, the grocer: rows of vegetables, the colors vivid,
the weight of each cabbage, the heft of it more solid, the weight against

each moment of memory: standing at the docks, scavenging for food, leaving
the dead, the weight of each choice. Now it is which vegetable is most fresh,

which cut of meat affordable, how far to stretch the food: a simple choice:
a planned outcome: a sure thing:

The soup will last three days.

The walk to the streetcar will take ten minutes.

There will be food in the store to buy.

The Chorus Considers The Fire

—Ash, sticky and sweet.

*—Smyrna continued to burn inside them, to subside to ash, embers, ash sticky
on the scaffolding, methylated, singing along the skeleton of their DNA:*

*the fire, the horse hooves, the running over the dead bodies of their sisters, brothers, friends,
children, the no-home, the hunger, the wailing, the cowering in the basement,
the days and nights on the quay, the fear, the no-food, the hunger, the starving,
the shame, the pleading, the no-hope, the boarding a boat for another
land with no hope, no place, no help, no money, no language:*

all ash, sticky, sweet, sickeningly sweet.

Thromos: there is a road. It is music, the bouzouki finding the path.

•

—The rebetis appeared to be law-abiding.

—The rebetis was a fighter.

—The rebetis smoked hashish.

—The rebetis safeguarded his personal freedom.

•

The players gather in the *cafenío*, one by one they wander in, sit in the corner. This one is a famous bouzouki player, the one on the movies, but here, he sits with his back to the tables. He wants to find the road. He wants to be alone. He is walking the steps down into the music. The hookah is passed but he keeps his hands on his instrument. He is finding the road and laying it down. Soon, the others will follow. They will join him on the journey. *Clarino, bouzouki, baglamas. Smyrna* style: Carried over the water. *Zeibekiko* rhythm: *Rembetika.*

•

—The rebetis spoke in slang.

—The rebetis loved shoes with a high heel, enough space for a mouse to pass under the arch.

—The rebetis protected those who had been wronged.

—The rebetis knew how to use a knife.

•

And here, someone rises: the old woman stands and sways, eyes closed,
      to dance *zembekiko*. Finger snap. Foot slide.

She sways
        for a few moments, sits down. At a table across the room, a young man

rises, swaying: *zembekiko*. Eyes closed. And over here, a grandfather. The young man

sinks back into his chair, the older woman rises again. They rise
        and dance in place, *zembekiko*: no regard for each other. Each one

listens to an internal voice, rises when the need pushes upward,
sits when the need is exhausted.

—When released.

•

—The rebetis was a member of the underworld.

—They carried the music with them:

—Rembetika: harsh, modal:
Rembetika: Smyna style: Smyrneiki:

—Carried over the water.

•

They are ghosts, who call

                         their losses to take shape in the room, who make the music
visible—*finger snap, sway*—rise and dance: *zembekiko*:

seeing only inside, finding the road, blind—

•

—No one applauds.

•

     —An architecture of injury (harm). A scaffolding on which to hang the cost.

The Chorus Considers Fate, Again & Again

—*And then you rotate under its weight.*

—*It will find you. Whatever you do will only bring it closer.*
—*This is your fate.*
Child.

—*Or too much written on it.*

Or nothing written on it.

—*Blank slate.*

—Katabasis: *a second going under:*
turn in the path, pulling underwater,
sweeping away.

—*You push back against it.*

—*(Of) being at the beck and call.*

—*This is your fate:*

—*Child.*
—*Child.*

Can a life be fitted to lamentation?

The way something has been hollowed out.

But what I want is of no consequence.

              —It means you are underwater while everyone else breathes air.

Or everything has shifted, just a slight skewing of the horizon line, the trees
and houses tilted slightly to the left.

                         —But what you want is of no consequence.

Just that fuzzy mental palette: all cotton, all fog.

When everyone else seems able to speak, able to believe in the words they say.

Able to make sense of the world, to believe some version of it.

                         —Able to use the future tense,
                 believe all the outlines will stay in place.

The Chorus Considers Epigenetics

Let me study your affliction:

Methyl groups attach to DNA for life—sticky pollen, falling ash, tracing the framework—
shifting the activity of the gene. Behavioral traits associated with those genes
also changed, likewise

cellular markers, a gift, sweet ash handed

transmitted across generations:

to each offspring.

The scent heavy in the mouth. ~~Not ash, sweet. But heavy.~~ *Methylation.*

Bruise. Ornament.

Ash.

The pressure of *now*: the tasks to be attended to more lovely, more necessary: small gestures: cutting the bread, having the bread to eat, making the meal, watching the child: each gesture driven by its underside, its ash, each gesture a salve, each task a stone in the wall being built daily, piece by piece.

—Even here the mind will not cooperate,
even here the world hands back images, again and again.

•

How many tasks to fall through before finding silence? How far to fall?

What filters each moment? What filters do the eyes look through?

How wide is the word *it?* How deep? How much can it hold?

How many tasks to fall through before finding silence? How far to fall?

AFTERWORD

A Short History of Anger takes as its source material the Destruction of Smyrna, in Asia Minor in 1922, and the resulting population exchange between the Greek and Turkish governments. What happened in Asia Minor in the early 1900s sowed the seeds for subsequent conflicts in Europe and helped set the stage for current issues in the Middle East. It was an important moment in history, and it involved many of the world's larger and smaller powers. The culture of the Ottoman Empire in Asia Minor, and specifically in Smyrna, was unlike any other culture before or since, and although some of the alliances were uneasy, it serves as a model of how people of disparate cultural backgrounds and religions can peacefully coexist. That culture no longer exists.

Smyrna was an international city, very different from mainland Greece at the time, its land richer, its culture more European. The Greek citizens took their cultural cues from France, rather than Greece. Made up primarily of Turks, Greeks, Armenians, and Jews, the city was cosmopolitan, known for "Smyrna style" and a particular *joie de vivre*, full of cafés, bars, ouzerias, with a strong culture of art, opera, music, dancing. *Rembetika* music—now the popular form of the blues in Greek culture—with its mix of eastern and western influences, originated in Smyrna. That mix—of western and Middle Eastern influence, in food, music, language, and culture—characterized the city. The population numbers are a matter of dispute, but the largest population was Greek, somewhere in the neighborhood of 175,000 people who made up mostly the middle and upper classes. Greeks were prosperous, and although second-class citizens as Ottoman subjects, they controlled trade and business, worked in many professions and were free to worship as they pleased. The second largest group were Turks, followed by Armenians (until 1915 or so) and a small population of Jews. They spoke each other's languages, in addition to French and Italian, were neighbors and friends and business associates, and identified by religion, rather than nationality: Muslim Ottoman subjects; Greek Orthodox Ottoman subjects. Culturally, the Greeks had more allegiance to Asia Minor than to Greece and many of their families had been living in Asia Minor for thousands of years.

The story is an ancient one, spanning centuries, but the events this book centers on began during World War I, when the British government asked Greece to help win the war for the Allies in Asia Minor in exchange for a return of territory, including

Smyrna. The Prime Minister of Greece, Eliftherios Venizelos, and Lloyd George, the Prime Minister of the Wartime Coalition Government in Britain, had a vision of a Greece with all its ancient territory restored—a plan called *The Great Idea*—that Greek citizens embraced.

After the war, the rising powers in Turkey, the Young Turks led by Mustapha Kemal, didn't recognize the treaty brokered by Britain and France, which granted territory, including Smyrna, to Greece, and restored a Hellenic empire on both sides of the Aegean (*The Great Idea*). Nor did they recognize the arriving Greek army, which pushed inland from Smyrna and set about destroying villages and laying claim to territory. The ensuing conflict ended in the Turkish army's takeover of Smyrna and the genocide of Smyrna's Greek citizens, known as The Destruction of Smyrna, or in Greece, simply as *The Catastrophe*. During the final years of the weakened Ottoman rule, the developing Turkish government had been executing a systematic ethnic cleansing of ethnic Christian minorities in Turkey: first the Armenians, then thousands of Greek citizens from inland Anatolia were exterminated. For weeks before the Destruction, Greek refugees from inland Anatolia had been streaming into Smyrna, fleeing the advancing Turkish army.

Few Greeks escaped the Destruction, as they were murdered or driven into the sea, literally, by the Turkish army; the British fleet (and French and American ships) at anchor in the harbor offered no refuge, claiming non-involvement. The atrocities committed by both the Greek and Turkish armies were brutal and senseless, but at this point, the Turkish intent to eradicate the Greek citizens reached a kind of fever pitch. Seeing the shift in power, the British government switched allegiances, planning on trade agreements with Turkey, including in oil, and abandoned the Greek citizens of Smyrna. The Turkish army and bands of mercenary soldiers set the Greek section of the city on fire, pillaged the city, raped and murdered the Greek citizens, and drove the refugees to the harbor, where thousands of them gathered along the quay. When the fire spread through the city, the refugees on the quay had nowhere to go but into the sea, where thousands of them drowned while the British fleet broadcast music to mask the sound of screaming.

Subsequently, there was a "population exchange" between the Greek and Turkish governments, supported by the Allies, in which all Orthodox Christians were moved to Greece and all Muslims to Turkey. In Turkey, Orthodox citizens were given five days to evacuate. We are still dealing with the fallout from this policy and its legacy, and the humanitarian nightmare it created—the scale of which was unprecedented. Families were broken apart, people who had lived peacefully together were forced from their homes, over a million refugees flooded Greece, overwhelming its resources and creating levels of antagonism between mainland Greeks and Asia Minor refugees. Thousands more people perished during the population exchange. There are many stories of Turkish people singing songs, packing food, and mourning for their neighbors being forced to flee; many stories of Greeks from Smyrna who still identify themselves as from Smyrna fifty years after the population exchange.

Oddly, the world has remained largely silent about these events and many people, certainly most Americans, know nothing about The Destruction or population exchange. But it became a blueprint for state-sponsored genocide and ethnic cleansing in Europe. Of particular significance was the switch from identification by religion to nationalism for these citizens, which has created much of the strife and hatred and desire for territory that have fueled the many wars of the 20th and 21st centuries.

Acknowledgments

Many thanks to the editors of journals that have published excerpts, under different titles, and to the producers who have sponsored staged readings of the manuscript, under the title *A Short History of Anger: A Hybrid Work of Poetry & Theatre*:

Ambit (London, UK): "A Short History of Anger: The Refugee as Double"

Voices Series, Plymouth University, Plymouth, UK: *A Short History of Anger: Staged Reading*

Transnational Creatives Festival, TRACE, Bath Spa University, Bath, UK: *A Short History of Anger: Staged Reading*

Theatre & English Departments, Holocaust Lecture Series, Vanderbilt University: *A Short History of Anger: A Hybrid Work of Poetry & Theatre*

Theatre & Creative Writing Departments, Frederick Loewe Theatre, University of Redlands: *A Short History of Anger: A Hybrid Work of Poetry & Theatre*

———————

A Short History of Anger exists as both book and performance. As this work came into being, the written and the performative informed each other and helped shape the final piece.

The writing came first. Many people sustained me through that long process. My gratitude to Maxine Scates, Molly Spencer, and Connie Voisine for their careful responses to the manuscript. To Eleanor Wilner, for reading early and then, again, in its final form. To Jennifer Sweeney for consultation and connection on all levels. To my poetry circle, Mary Ann McFadden, Jennifer Sweeney, Youna Kwak and to friends Sara Schoonmaker, Pat Geary, and Eli Andrew Ramer for belief and cheering on. Max, again, for walking this terrain with me. Πολλές ευχαριστίες to Nephelie and Avyeris Andonyadis, also from Asia Minor, who consulted on all things Greek. For a space to work and belief in its necessity, endless gratitude to Sybil Heidel Bigley, whose spirit stays with me.

To my family of origin—those who perished and those who escaped The Destruction—your voices lifted me up. And especially my cousin, Jenny Sessions, who recounted the experience over many hours of time together. And my mother, Catherine Caloyer Mason, who first suggested I investigate Smyrna and whose family story weaves through this piece. To both I owe a debt of gratitude. To my grandmother, Iro Plittas Caloyer, who survived The Destruction, and modeled how to meet fear with laughter.

To those who assisted in bringing the book into the world: deep gratitude to Brenda Hillman and Jon Thompson for their wide palettes, for seeing the work and understanding its enterprise. And to David Blakesley, for all his work at Parlor Press. And to Margaret Buchanan, my sister in art, for the countless hours of her attention and her graceful design.

———————————

A host of people assisted in shaping the many performances of *A Short History of Anger*.

Bambo Soyinka and Adnan Mahmutovic, whose insight created the amazing community at the first *International Symposium for Transnational Creative Practice*, in Stockholm, Sweden. And to colleagues at the symposium who helped me first see the piece as spoken aloud by many voices. Special thanks to Bambo Soyinka, for her friendship, her imagination, and her welcome into that community.

A Short History of Anger would not have been realized as a performance without the vision and guiding force of Chris Beach, who understood its hybrid nature, saw possibilities I could not see, and magicked the performance to life, in its many iterations. The first Chorus helped create the initial production, and especially, Steve Morics, who shaped the lament, and has been the pillar around which several different Choruses have circled. Thanks to Lucy Durneen, for bringing us to Plymouth. And deep gratitude to Sandy Solomon, friend and fellow poet, who opened the path for a performance at Vanderbilt University, and then assisted every step of the way. And of course, profound thanks to all the Chorus members, singers, and tech crews across the globe—too numerous to list here—who put in time, effort, and talent to conjure the work on stage.

——————————————

And finally, loving thanks to Chris and Zoë,
for their grace and laughter, and for all of it, every day.

——————————————

This book is dedicated to—and in memory of—essential friend, visionary poet, Brigit Pegeen Kelly, who first believed in this work and its possibility. I can't imagine my life without the buoy and sustenance of our long years of friendship and exchange. May her memory be eternal.

Ζωή σε εμάς.

Notes

George Seferis, the great Greek poet who was awarded the Nobel Prize in Literature in 1963, was a contemporary of my grandmother's in Smyrna. The Destruction was the determining historical event of his life, as noted by Walter Kaiser in the Introduction to *A Poet's Journal: Days of 1945—1951* (Cambridge: Harvard University Press, 1974). In 1948, Sepheris was posted to the Greek Embassy in Ankara, and in 1950, he returned to Smyrna for the first time. One section of his journal records his reflections during this return.

∎

The Chorus Considers the City Before the Destruction and
The Chorus Considers the City Before the Destruction, Again

Some of the details of culture, spoken text, and information in The Chorus sections were drawn from family oral histories and other sources, including Giles Milton's wonderful book, *Paradise Lost: Smyrna 1922*, (New York: Basic Books, 2008) about the Levantine community in Smryna, which makes that community come alive again.

∎

Ζωή σε εμάς = life to us, all who are living: In Greek culture, this phrase is said to people who have lost someone, and includes us all, all who mourn, who are together here now. It recognizes the community sharing in the grief and mourning.

May her/his/their memory be eternal: αιωνία η μνήμη is part of the Mnimosino Liturgy, the 40-day memorial service, chanted by priest and cantor. It is also said, in English, to mourners and survivors as a way to honor the deceased.

∎

The Chorus Considers the Matter of Numbers

The statistics on the numbers are in dispute, and here, are compiled from many sources, including Bruce Clark's *Twice a Stranger: The Mass Expulsions that Forged Modern Greece and Turkey* (Cambridge, Massachusetts: Harvard University Press, 2006) and the film of the same name; Marjorie Housepian Dobkin's *Smyrna 1922: The Destruction of a City*, (New York: Newmark Press, 1972); Consul and Consul General of the United States in the Near East, George Horton's, account of The Destruction, *The Blight of Asia*; and Giles Milton's *Paradise Lost* (mentioned above). Family members also gave opinions and ideas on the populations of Smyrna.

∎

The Chorus Considers the Population Exchange and
The Chorus Considers the Population Exchange, Again

Most of these statements are quotes or paraphrases from interviews on Bruce Clark's film, *Twice a Stranger*, Anemon, EPT, and Prisma+, 2012., as well as from family oral histories.

∎

Thromos: there is a road. It is music, the bouzouki finding the path.

Gayle Holst's book, *Road to Rembetika* (Limni and Athens, Greece: Denise Harvey & Co, 1975) was very helpful in providing context and information about *rembetika* music. Asia Minor refugees carried *rembetika* from Smyrna, a form of music much like the blues that blends Greek and Turkish influences so reminiscent of Smyrna's unique culture. Through *rembetika*, people expressed their pain, the unspeakable sorrow of displacement, and their longing for home. In Smyrna, *rembetika* was embraced by many levels of society, but when it moved to mainland Greece, *rembetika* became associated with an urban lifestyle and it became popular in the hashish dens along the ports. A *rebetis,* also known as a *mangas,* was someone who embraced the *rembetiko* lifestyle, which included both a code of honor and a particular code of presentation: hats, mustaches, and certain verbal mannerisms. Often thought of as gangsters, many of them were involved in gambling, drinking, and drugs, but they also had an anti-establishment ethos and they created *rembetika* wherever they went.

The Chorus Considers Epigenetics

Research into epigenetics—heritable changes in gene expression—over the past decade has posited the notion that trauma can be passed genetically through generations by methyl groups' attachment to the DNA within cells. There are many articles in mainstream literature, including in *Scientific American, The Guardian*, and *The New York Time*s, that describe the research and changes in the field, some of which is in dispute. Dan Hurley's article, "Grandma's Experiences Leave a Mark on Your Genes," in the June 25, 2015 issue of *Discover* magazine is helpful as entry into the research.

ABOUT THE AUTHOR

 Joy Manesiotis is the author of *They Sing to Her Bones*, which won the New Issues Poetry Prize. Recently, she has staged *A Short History of Anger: A Hybrid Work of Poetry & Theatre*—comprised of a Speaker and Greek Chorus— at international festivals and universities in the US and Europe. Poems and essays have appeared widely in literary journals and anthologies, including *The American Poetry Review*, *Poetry*, *Massachusetts Review*, *Virginia Quarterly Review*, and *Poetry International*, as well as in translation, in the Romanian journal, *Scrisul Romanesc*. Manesiotis has received fellowships from *New York Foundation for the Arts*, the Graves Award, and Ragdale Foundation, and her poems were dropped over Nicosia, Cyprus as part of *Spring Poetry Rain*, an international cultural event to help foster peace in the last divided city in Europe. She is the Edith R. White Distinguished Professor Emerita in Creative Writing, University of Redlands and serves on the editorial board of Airlie Press.

Free Verse Editions

Edited by Jon Thompson

13 ways of happily by Emily Carr
& in Open, Marvel by Felicia Zamora
& there's still you thrill hour of the world to love by Aby Kaupang
Alias by Eric Pankey
At Your Feet (A Teus Pés) by Ana Cristina César,
    edited by Katrina Dodson, trans. by Brenda Hillman and Helen Hillman
Bari's Love Song by Kang Eun-Gyo, translated by Chung Eun-Gwi
Between the Twilight and the Sky by Jennie Neighbors
Blood Orbits by Ger Killeen
The Bodies by Christopher Sindt
The Book of Isaac by Aidan Semmens
The Calling by Bruce Bond
Canticle of the Night Path by Jennifer Atkinson
Child in the Road by Cindy Savett
Civil Twilight by Giles Goodland
Condominium of the Flesh by Valerio Magrelli,
    trans. by Clarissa Botsford Contrapuntal by Christopher Kondrich
Country Album by James Capozzi
Cry Baby Mystic by Daniel Tiffany
The Curiosities by Brittany Perham
Current by Lisa Fishman
Day In, Day Out by Simon Smith
Dear Reader by Bruce Bond
Dismantling the Angel by Eric Pankey
Divination Machine by F. Daniel Rzicznek
Elsewhere, That Small by Monica Berlin
Empire by Tracy Zeman
Erros by Morgan Lucas Schuldt
Fifteen Seconds without Sorrow by Shim Bo-Seon,
    trans. by Chung Eun-Gwi and Brother Anthony of Taizé
The Forever Notes by Ethel Rackin
The Flying House by Dawn-Michelle Baude
General Release from the Beginning of the World by Donna Spruijt-Metz
Ghost Letters by Baba Badji
Go On by Ethel Rackin

Here City by Rick Snyder
Instances: Selected Poems by Jeongrye Choi,
    trans. by Brenda Hillman, Wayne de Fremery & Jeongrye Choi
Last Morning by Simon Smith
The Magnetic Brackets by Jesús Losada, trans. by M. Smith & L. Ingelmo
Man Praying by Donald Platt
A Map of Faring by Peter Riley
The Miraculous Courageous by Josh Booton
Mirrorforms by Peter Kline
A Myth of Ariadne by Martha Ronk
No Shape Bends the River So Long by Monica Berlin & Beth Marzoni
North\Rock\Edge by Susan Tichy
Not into the Blossoms and Not into the Air by Elizabeth Jacobson
Overyellow by Nicolas Pesquès, translated by Cole Swensen
Parallel Resting Places by Laura Wetherington
pH of Au by Vanessa Couto Johnson
Physis by Nicolas Pesquès, translated by Cole Swensen
Pilgrimage Suites by Derek Gromadzki
Pilgrimly by Siobhán Scarry
Poems from above the Hill & Selected Work by Ashur Etwebi,
    trans. by Brenda Hillman & Diallah Haidar
The Prison Poems by Miguel Hernández, trans. by Michael Smith
Puppet Wardrobe by Daniel Tiffany
Quarry by Carolyn Guinzio
remanence by Boyer Rickel
Republic of Song by Kelvin Corcoran
Rumor by Elizabeth Robinson
Settlers by F. Daniel Rzicznek
A Short History of Anger by Joy Manesiotis
Signs Following by Ger Killeen
Small Sillion by Joshua McKinney
Split the Crow by Sarah Sousa
Spine by Carolyn Guinzio
Spool by Matthew Cooperman
Strange Antlers by Richard Jarrette
A Suit of Paper Feathers by Nate Duke
Summoned by Guillevic, trans. by Monique Chefdor & Stella Harvey

Sunshine Wound by L. S. Klatt
System and Population by Christopher Sindt
These Beautiful Limits by Thomas Lisk
They Who Saw the Deep by Geraldine Monk
The Thinking Eye by Jennifer Atkinson
This History That Just Happened by Hannah Craig
An Unchanging Blue: Selected Poems 1962-1975 by Rolf Dieter Brinkmann,
    trans. by Mark Terrill
Under the Quick by Molly Bendall
Verge by Morgan Lucas Schuldt
The Visible Woman by Allison Funk
The Wash by Adam Clay
We'll See by Georges Godeau, trans. by Kathleen McGookey
What Stillness Illuminated by Yermiyahu Ahron Taub
Winter Journey [Viaggio d'inverno] by Attilio Bertolucci,
    trans. by Nicholas Benson
Wonder Rooms by Allison Funk

CPSIA information can be obtained
at www.ICGtesting.com
Printed in the USA
JSHW060911070123
35754JS00002B/3

"JOY MANESIOTIS is a brilliant poet, one who understands, that lyric, as Joseph Brodsky once insisted, is a soul's release into language. So, watch how the line-breaks, sentences, precise orchestrations and wonders of syntax work in her poems, how they move us to a different register of human emotions, how they open doors we did not know exist. Manesiotis is wonder poet, one whose work I admire deeply." —**Ilya Kaminsky**, author of *Dancing In Odessa* and *Deaf Republic*

"When a great catastrophe, the genocide of the Greeks of Smyrna, is immured in silence, does collective horror harbor in the genes—the blood line a long fuse smoldering with hidden fire, 'Smyrna burning and burning....' How to speak of such things? But 'who will sing the *moirolaia* to help the souls cross over?' In answer, voices—ancestral, choral, personal—rise from the ashes in this eloquent *moirolaia* of Joy Manesiotis: recovered history, lamentation, remembrance, release." —**Eleanor Wilner**, author of *Before Our Eyes: New and Selected Poems, 1975–2017*

"When, in Anna Akhmatova's famous poem, she was asked 'Can you describe this?' about an atrocity she lived through, she replied, 'Yes, I can.' In *A Short History of Anger*, Joy Manesiotis lifts the same burden of responsibility to her own shoulders, and the beautiful, heartbreaking poem she made here could have been written a thousand years ago, or yesterday. And the terrible thing is, when I look up from this book, our landscape is the same as inside it: on fire. When no remedy is coming, poets at least make it possible to sit in the dirt and weep. Sit here with me. I would count it a privilege to hold your hand and keen these poems together." —**Patrick Donnelly**, author of *Little-Known Operas*, *Nocturnes of the Brothel of Ruin*, and *The Charge*

JOY MANESIOTIS is the author of *They Sing to Her Bones*, which won the New Issues Poetry Prize. Recently, she has staged *A Short History of Anger: A Hybrid Work of Poetry & Theatre*—comprised of a Speaker and Greek Chorus—at international festivals and universities in the US and Europe.

PARLOR PRESS

EQUIPMENT FOR LIVING

3015 Brackenberry Drive
Anderson, South Carolina 29621
www.parlorpress.com
SAN 254-8879
ISBN 978-1-64317-367-2

ISBN 978-1-64317-367-2
90000
9 781643 173672